THE ROLLING STONES

" QUOTE UNQUOTE "

THE ROLLING STONES

" QUOTE UNQUOTE "

Jon Ewing

PARRAGON

PICTURE CREDITS

Redferns: 33, 51, 66; David Redfern 8, 15, 23, 45, 46, 48, 65; Alex Korner 11; Bob Vincett 12;
Michael Ochs Archive 28; Bob King 30; Glenn A. Baker 31; C. Andrews 34, 43; Graham Wiltshire
37, 72; Peter Sanders 52; Ebet Roberts 53, 79; Richie Aaron 54, 61, 74; Mick Hutson 77;
Retna: © King Collection 6, 10, 12, 13, 14, 16, 18, 19, 27; © Michael Putland Front Cover, Back
Cover, 2, 24, 39, 40, 49, 62, 64, 68, 71; © Mark Anderson 60; © Luciano Viti 75;
© Rocky Widner 77

Every effort has been made to trace the copyright holders and we apologize in advance for any
unintentional omissions. We would be pleased to insert the appropriate acknowledgement in any
subsequent edition of this publication.

First published in Great Britain in 1996 by
Parragon Book Service Ltd
Unit 13–17
Avonbridge Trading Estate
Atlantic Road
Avonmouth
Bristol BS11 9QD

Copyright © Parragon Book Service Ltd 1996

ISBN: 0-7525-1604-3

Produced by Haldane Mason, London

Editor: Paul Barnett
Design: Digital Artworks Partnership Ltd
Picture Research: Charles Dixon-Spain

Printed in Italy

CONTENTS

OH BABY
(WE GOT A GOOD THING GOIN')

'Performing's like sex. You
might like it, but you don't wanna
do it all the time.'
MICK

FACING PAGE: *While the Beatles were cheeky and chirpy,*
the Stones were always moody and magnificent.

Destiny brought them together. Michael Jagger and Keith Richards were born in Dartford, Kent, in 1943 and lived just a few streets apart. They attended the same primary school and sat in the same classroom, but for the first 18 years of their lives they were all but strangers.

ABOVE: Mick was never a conventionally handsome boy.

'I used to pose in front of the mirror at home. I was hopeful. The only thing I was lacking was a bit of bread to buy an instrument. But I got the moves off first, and I got the guitar later.' KEITH

'I asked him what he wanted to do when he grew up,' recalled Jagger many years later. 'He said he wanted to be a cowboy like Roy Rogers and play a guitar. I wasn't that impressed by Roy Rogers, but the bit about the guitar *did* interest me.'

Mick Jagger's father, Basil Joe, was a physical-training teacher and one of Britain's earliest exponents of basketball. Mick's mother Eva had emigrated to Britain from Australia in her teens. The family lived in Denver Road, Dartford, deep in the suburban south of London. As a boy he was known as Mike. A diligent lad who shared his father's talent for sports, he earned a place at the respectable Dartford Grammar School. His academic success continued throughout his teenage years, but during this time Mike Jagger began to metamorphose from a chubby, spirited schoolboy into a gaunt, brooding young man with sharp cheekbones and thick, pouting lips. He disobeyed the school's dress regulations and, before the dismayed gaze of his once-approving teachers, grew increasingly apathetic. The young Jagger had been captivated by something more diverting than cricket, maths or the army cadets: the Blues.

The Skiffle craze had swept the nation, and teenagers everywhere were banging out tuneless versions of watered-down Blues songs on washboard, guitar and tea-chest bass, but Mike Jagger took little interest in this degraded version. Nor did he care much for the crooning of Elvis Presley or Bill Haley. He and his friend Dick Taylor were interested only in the real thing. In March 1958 they travelled together to Woolwich to see Buddy Holly on his first and only British tour. Holly was then at the cutting edge of rock'n'roll, helping to create not just a new genre but a new culture of popular music. Everything about him – including the way he looked – was unconventional. Jagger was entranced by the white singer's black R&B style, mixing with a Texas Country & Western twang a disenfranchised 'race' music which had never been heard in Britain before. Inspired, the boys soon formed a four-piece band called Little Boy Blue & The Blue Boys, which regularly practised at Dick's house. They searched out original American Blues records and tried

---

'We were popping pills, then to stay awake without sleep more than to get high. We used to buy these nose inhalers called Nostrilene, for the benzedrine, or even take girls' period pills. Opposite the college, there was this little park with an aviary that had a cockatoo in it. Cocky the Cockatoo we used to call it. Keith used to feed it pep pills and make it stagger around on the perch. If ever we were feeling bored, we'd go and give another upper to Cocky the Cockatoo.' DICK TAYLOR ON COLLEGE LIFE WITH KEITH.

---

to produce their own versions; often they sent away to America for the newest and best. The rarity of the records was part of their appeal – to these Kentish

ABOVE: Keith was a tearaway in his teens.

One day, on his regular train journey to the city, he spotted a face from the past: Keith Richards. The two teenagers from different sides of the tracks made an odd couple, but Richards was impressed by Jagger's armful of rare Blues records, and in those few minutes between Dartford and Sidcup they discovered a mutual passion. Before they went their separate ways, Jagger invited Richards to come over and audition for The Blue Boys. The performance was a revelation – on his semisolid Hofner cutaway, Richards was already a budding guitar hero, playing with style and ease. He was welcomed into the group at once.

Keith Richards was a scruffy, wolfish-faced teenager with few academic prospects. After their brief period sharing the same primary school, the boys might have grown up together had not Richards's parents Doris and Bert moved away to live on a housing estate on the other side of Dartford. In the intervening years, Jagger had become a middle-class undergraduate with pseudo-intellectual opinions and 'bohemian' clothes. Richards, on the other hand, was a Teddy Boy, dressed in tight blue jeans and winklepicker shoes. He had developed a hostility towards authority, both at school and at home.

teenagers, rock'n'roll was a fantasy offering escape into an unimaginably exotic world. Little Boy Blue & The Blue Boys never thought of playing in front of an audience – it never occurred to them that anyone else might understand their love affair with the Blues. They were in a world of their own.

Jagger's academic aspirations had long ago dissipated, yet he gained a place at the London School of Economics, beginning his studies there in 1961. 'I wanted to do arts, but I thought I ought to do science,' he recalled later. 'Economics seemed about halfway in between.'

Pampered by his mother and tolerated lovingly by his hard-working father, he had spent his schooldays as a persistent truant, dedicating every possible waking hour to playing the guitar and listening to his growing collection of R&B records. Eventually expelled from school, he had wound up at Sidcup Art College – the last stop for an incorrigible student before the inevitable arrival at the dole queue. Consequently his future looked pretty bleak . . . until that accidental meeting with Jagger on an early-morning commuter train changed his life forever.

In March 1962, Mick – as he now liked to call himself – and the other Blue Boys drove to Ealing, in London, to see Britain's first recognized Blues band, Alexis Korner's Blues Incorporated. At each session, this band invited enthusiastic amateurs to join them on stage. Accordingly, inspired by the show and heartened by Korner's encouragement, Mick returned the following week. Terrified and half-drunk, he stepped on stage to sing for the first time in public – a version of Chuck Berry's 'Around and Around'. Korner recognized, behind Jagger's stage fright, a true passion for the music and a soulful rhythm in the youth's movements. From that night onwards, Jagger became a member of Korner's band, acting as understudy to full-time vocalist Long John Baldry. The Blue Boys regularly travelled to London on Saturdays to visit the Ealing club, often stopping off at Korner's home to talk interminably about American Blues heroes.

It was at one of Korner's shows that they were first introduced to Brian Jones.

Jones was a dark horse. A talented multi-instrumentalist and a promising student at Cheltenham Grammar School, he had discovered jazz, and the

BELOW: Alex Korner's Blues Incorporated.

ABOVE: At first, Brian Jones was the acknowledged leader of the Stones.

and was himself a skilled alto-sax player – but most of all he craved the adulation of celebrity. In 1961 his latest girlfriend gave birth to a son, Julian, and Jones set off to make his fortune in London, with the poor girl following devotedly behind.

Taking on a job in a department store, Jones dedicated himself to forming a Blues band which would take the world by storm. He bought a Gibson guitar and rechristened himself Elmo Lewis – after the Blues legend Elmore James. In Oxford he met Paul Pond – later to become Paul Jones, lead singer of the

alternative lifestyle that went with it, at the age of 14. His deliberate efforts to build up a reputation as a troublemaker – despite his successful academic qualifications – ended when a pregnant 14-year-old revealed that Jones was responsible for her condition. The baby was put out for adoption and Jones was asked to leave the school. He took on various unskilled jobs – his passion for buses led him to take a brief traineeship with Cheltenham Municipal Transport – but the one constant since his early teens had been music. He idolized Charlie Parker,

BELOW: The early Stones had idealistic dreams of bringing Blues to the masses.

'I owned a Vox AC–30 amplifier, which was really something in those days. It was . . . quite a valuable asset. So they thought, "Oh, really good amp; bass player's nothing special, but we'll keep him so we can use the amp." That was the general opinion, I have since learned. You know, they are real con artists, that lot.' BILL

group Manfred Mann — and together they earned a support slot with Alexis Korner's Blues Incorporated in Ealing. After the show, Jagger and Richards introduced themselves to 'Elmo', and together they talked about Blues for the rest of the evening. A few days later, Jones formed a new band: himself and Keith Richards on guitar, Dick Taylor on bass, Mick Jagger on vocals and new-comer Ian 'Stew' Stewart on piano; it would be some time before they could settle on a regular drummer. They prac-tised three times a week in the back room of a London pub until, on July 12, 1962, they were offered their first gig, at London's Marquee Club. Jones named the band the Rollin' Stones, after the Muddy Waters song — a choice that was not altogether popular with the rest of the line-up.

The show was a partial success. The hardcore jazz audience was defiantly opposed to the rock'n'roll influences of Chuck Berry and Bo Diddley, but the Mods in the crowd gave them a good reception. The club's manager, Harold Pendleton, offered them a few more spots. In the meantime Jagger, Jones and Richards moved into a squalid two-room bedsit in Edith Grove, Chelsea. Jones and

LEFT: *No one realized until years later that Bill was the 'Old Man' of the Stones.*

'I was nineteen when it started to take off, right, and just a very ordinary guy. Chucked out of nightclubs, birds'd poke their tongues out at me, that kind of scene. And then, suddenly, Adonis! And you know, that is so ridiculous, so totally insane.' KEITH

Richards were out of work and the three survived on Jagger's LSE grant and food parcels sent from Kent by Keith's mother.

The Marquee bookings ended when Richards picked a fight with Pendleton, but fortunately Stew owned a van and was able to drive the band to gigs further afield. They played pubs and clubs every weekend, building up a regular following in Richmond, Twickenham and the more remote London suburbs. The rest of the week they spent in bed, too poor to go out or even to feed the electricity meter. 'We'd spend hours at a time just making faces at each other,' recalls Keith.

As 1962 came to a close, Dick Taylor decided that he could no longer pin his hopes on a life as a musician, and left the band to study at the Royal College of Art. His replacement was Bill Perks, also known as Bill Wyman; a semi-professional musician, seven years older than Mick and Keith, Wyman was already married and had a son. Although less than impressed by the band and its prospects, he decided to give it a try. 'Despite all the sordid and chaotic circumstances,' he confesses, 'I was strangely drawn to the Stones.'

LEFT: Charlie never expected the Rolling Stones to succeed.

Drummer Charlie Watts joined the line-up with similar misgivings. 'Lots of my friends thought I'd gone raving mad,' he admits. A Londoner born and bred, Watts had a good job with a London advertising agency, and had also been playing with professional groups — including Korner's Blues Incorporated — for some time. The Rollin' Stones offered no future but, as Watts had anyway made up his mind to concentrate on his career as a commercial artist, he went along for the ride, expecting nothing more than fun.

By February 1963, however, the band was attracting big crowds on Sunday nights at the Crawdaddy Club, in Richmond. The audience was a cross-section of London nightlife, from smart-suited Mods to leather-clad Rockers and 'bohemian' students. The club's promoter, Giorgio Gomelsky, was so pleased with the Stones that he became their first manager. 'It was always a *partnership*,' he insists. 'I used to divide the door receipts equally with them. They would help me keep the club going . . . we never paid to advertise the Crawdaddy Club. The Stones and I would put illegal fly-posters all over. I got them printed for £4 a thousand and the Stones mixed up the paste in the bath at Edith Grove.'

On Sunday April 14, 1963 Giorgio invited the Beatles — about to top the charts for the first time with 'From Me To You' — to the Crawdaddy. The two groups became good friends from that night on, little knowing that between them they would change the face of popular music forever.

Meanwhile, Andrew Loog Oldham, a fast-talking, 19-year-old music publicist, was carving his own niche in the history of pop. Oldham, the illegitimate son of a Dutchman who had been serving in the US Air Force, was a dreamer, full of get-rich-quick schemes. Only a total lack of musical aptitude had prevented him from becoming a pop star. The next best

ABOVE: The Stones became a five-piece when their pianist was demoted to road manager.

thing, he supposed, was to be a pop impresario, mingling with the rich and powerful. He had used his slippery tongue and unashamed persistence to shape himself a career as press agent for Brian Epstein's NEMS Enterprises. When his contract with NEMS suddenly ended, Oldham went out to look for something new. His search took him to the Crawdaddy Club, and his shrewd nose for fashion spotted the next big thing. 'I knew what I was looking at,' he remembers. 'It was sex. And I was just ahead of the pack.'

Taking advantage of Giorgio Gomelsky's absence, Oldham approached Brian Jones – the group's apparent leader – and proposed himself as their new manager. They were impressed. 'Andrew talked the same way we did and wore the same clothes,' Bill Wyman explains. 'He seemed to care about what we cared about – just the Blues and getting it better known in Britain.'

In fact, Oldham's principal goal was to make *himself* better known. He had no real hope of offering the Stones the future he promised unless he could find a financial backer. The following week, he cajoled established London agent Eric Easton down to Richmond to witness the birth of a scruffy R&B phenomenon. Easton was hardly thrilled, particularly by Jagger's affected voice, but he recognized the same qualities Oldham had spotted, and agreed to put up the money.

By May 1963 the word was out. A feature in *Record Mirror* – which was highly influential in the music trade – predicted that the Rolling Stones (as they were now known) would become 'the biggest group in the R&B scene'. On the personal recommendation of Beatles guitarist George Harrison, Decca's head A&R (Artiste & Repertoire) man Dick Rowe went to the Crawdaddy to see the act which might salvage his sagging

BELOW: The Stones were never afraid to sell themselves for fame.

reputation. Within a few days, Decca and the Rolling Stones had signed a recording contract.

Almost immediately, Oldham proved himself a headstrong business associate – a persona he later described as a 'nasty little upstart tycoon shit'. Fashioning himself as a British Phil Spector – the American record producer who had become more famous than the artists he recorded – Oldham insisted on over-seeing the band's first recording himself, although he knew nothing at all about record production. Both Decca and the Stones agreed that the results were unus-able, and the songs were recorded all over again from scratch at Decca's own recording studios.

The first Rolling Stones single, 'Come On', was a Chuck Berry cover; it had been in the Stones' repertoire since the beginning. On the day of its release, Oldham and Easton launched the band to the public via the top-rated television show *Thank Your Lucky Stars*, although not without a few compromises. First, and most important, Oldham felt that Stew's sensible, thick-set face was 'too normal', and relegated him to the position of road manager, carrying equipment and driving the band from town to town. Second, he

'This is a bit like getting ready to go off with the family to the seaside. You have to be sure to have a wee, first.'
BILL, ON PREPARING TO GO ON STAGE.

decided – for no adequately explained reason – that Keith Richards should drop the 's' from the end of his surname, pre-sumably in imitation of Cliff Richard. Meanwhile, Easton dressed the five sur-viving Stones in matching hound's-tooth check suits with velvet collars. They appeared and felt uncomfortable, but fitted the contemporary formula for success – they looked *clean*. Similarly, 'Come On' sounded like a stiffly conven-tional transcription of the original, but at the time it hinted at just sufficient rebel-lion to take it to Number 21 in the British charts.

The Stones were on their way.

Through the summer of 1963 the Rolling Stones played town-hall dances through-out the south and east of England, from Windsor to King's Lynn, Wisbech to

Margate. In September, thanks to Eric Easton, they joined a package tour of provincial cinemas which starred Fifties chart-toppers the Everly Brothers and cult R&B stars Bo Diddley and Little Richard. The tour took the Stones as far north as Liverpool, Newcastle and even Glasgow. 'A few miles out, and it was all new to me,' admits Keith. 'Up to then, I'd never been further north than London.'

The tour was a slow trudge from one shabby hotel to the next, playing twice nightly with rudimentary sound equip-

BELOW: The Stones rarely smiled or even looked into the camera in their moody portraits.

ment. Oldham — setting a pattern for the rest of his relations with the band — was conspicuous by his absence. Without any management presence to keep them on the straight and narrow, the Stones discarded their stage suits in favour of ruffled shirts or polo necks, corduroys and white jeans. By the standards of the conservatively presented musicians of the day, the Rolling Stones were the scruffiest band ever to have got up on a stage.

'I had heard of the Stones, obviously, but I didn't particularly like them. I preferred the Beatles and jazz.'
ASTRID, BILL'S SECOND WIFE

Oldham, meanwhile, was busy selecting a song to improve upon the success of 'Come On'. He booked the band into Decca's studios to record a version of the 1959 Coasters hit 'Poison Ivy', but it just didn't sound right. Oldham sorted through a myriad of Tin Pan Alley tunes looking for one which the Stones could make their own. Then, by luck, he bumped into John Lennon and Paul McCartney in London's Soho and – in a moment of typical generosity – they offered him a new song which they had just written. Shortly after the Stones' first arduous tour had finished, 'I Wanna Be Your Man' reached Number 12 in the charts. Although more pop than R&B, the single proved that the Stones were capable of a raw, aggressive sound that was new to British music. The trademark bottleneck slide guitar of Brian Jones and the thumping bass line from Bill Wyman were far dirtier and more down-to-earth than anything the Beatles had so far achieved.

Oldham – craving the potential publishing royalties – was determined that the next single by the Stones should be an original composition, but this was not to be. Jones, despite his undoubted versatility as a musician, was unable to conjure up even the simplest three-chord pop tune. On the other hand, the first material written jointly by Jagger and Richard showed commercial promise, but did not have the hard edge required for a Rolling Stones track. (Indeed, the first Jagger–Richard composition to have Top Ten success, 'That Girl Belongs to Yesterday', was recorded not by the

Stones but by Gene Pitney as his follow-up to 'Twenty-Four Hours From Tulsa'; it reached Number Seven in the charts in March 1964.)

In the event, the third Stones single was another old favourite, a version of 'Not Fade Away', which had been written by Buddy Holly and his producer Norman Petty way back in 1957. Reputedly taped at the culmination of a drunken studio party in January 1964, the track featured backing vocals by Phil

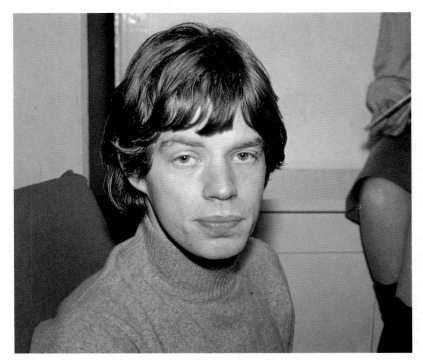

BELOW: Mick soon learned to live the life of a wealthy London socialite.

'Being on the road every night, you can tell by the way gigs are going, there's something enormous coming . . . You feel it winding tighter and tighter until one day you get out there halfway through the first number and the whole stage is full of chicks screaming "Nyeehhh!"' MICK

Spector and Gene Pitney, plus Graham Nash and Allan Clarke of the Hollies. The infectious, shuffling rhythm of the original combined with Jagger's brazen yell of youthful rebellion added up to make the track a massive hit. In the middle of the band's third national tour, the single reached Number Three in the charts. 'They look like boys whom any self-respecting mum would lock in the bathroom,' explained the *Daily Express*. 'But the Rolling Stones – five tough young London-based music-makers with doorstep mouths, pallid cheeks and unkempt hair – are not worried what mum thinks . . . For now that the Beatles have registered with all age groups, the Rolling Stones have taken over as the voice of the teens.'

Thanks to Oldham's over-active imagination, the Stones were becoming a threat to the Establishment, a potent symbol of misguided teenage morals. The scene of screaming girls crushed against police barriers was already a familiar one, but the Rolling Stones were far more surly and menacing than the Beatles. Their worst crime against common decency was the length and untidiness of their hair. In truth, Jones for one groomed his hair religiously, earning the nickname Shampoo, but he and the band wallowed in the controversy. 'We know a lot of people don't like us,' said Mick, ''cos they say we're scruffy and don't wash. So what? They don't have to come and look at us, do they?'

Mick relished his role as a pop star, introducing himself to London's fashionable upper echelons and being seen around with Chrissie Shrimpton, younger sister of *Vogue* model Jean. He, Keith and Oldham were now sharing a small flat in Willesden, North London, and learning to enjoy their success as they mixed in the more exclusive clubs. Jones had by now cut himself off completely from his family and the mother of his son Julian.

Before long his latest girlfriend was pregnant with his third child, and in time he would desert her, too, seeking fulfilment in the adoration of more chic and sophisticated women.

In April 1964 the first Rolling Stones album was released. As a bold and egotistical statement dreamed up by Andrew Loog Oldham, the front of the sleeve featured neither the band's name nor any title, merely the faces of the five, broody wunderkinder, their eyes indifferently glancing toward the camera. On the back, Oldham's notes proclaimed that the Stones were 'more than a group. They are a way of life.'

Summing up their career to date, the material was essentially a distillation of the band's overworked live set, with cover versions of American R&B standards like Marvin Gaye's 'Can I Get a Witness', Nat 'King' Cole's 'Route 66' and Chuck Berry's 'Carol'. Their own material was 'terrible', as Jagger now admits. The only Jagger–Richard song credit on the album was the sentimental and slushy 'Tell Me', although Phelge (a nom-de-plume chosen as an in-joke — it referred to a former flatmate) was noted as the contributor of two filler tracks. The long-awaited album notched up 100,000 in advance sales, and shot to Number One in the charts, displacing the phenomenally successful *With the Beatles*.

The Stones' next tour of Britain, the following month, was a riotous success — in some cases, literally. *New Musical Express* noted that the Stones were already poised to eclipse the hysteria created by

---

'Everyone we really hated seemed to be doing far better in the States than we were. They'd had a Number One record, done a good tour, good TV. We'd got nothing like that to look forward to. No wonder we were depressed on the way over.'

BILL, ON THE FIRST TRIP TO THE USA

---

the Beatles. 'From the moment Mick Jagger picked up his maracas and the Rolling Stones burst into action,' wrote Richard Green, 'it was a battle between them and the teenagers as to who could make the most noise.'

In America the album was subtitled *England's Newest Hitmakers* and included an additional track, 'Not Fade Away', absent from the British original. Stories of the band's hell-raising preceded them as they set off for America in June. 'The Stones have a perverse, unsettling sex appeal,' promised Diana Vreeland in *Vogue*, and she described Jagger as fascinating to women and intimidating to men. 'Quite different from the Beatles, and more terrifying,' she concluded. The American media in general regarded them either as a curiosity or not at all. Likewise, the crowds made them work hard for their applause and, to conservative music fans, the band's scruffy appearance was sinfully inappropriate for professional entertainers. 'I've never been hated by so many people I've never met as in Nebraska in the mid-Sixties,' claims Keith. 'Everyone looked at you with a look that could kill. You could tell they just wanted to beat the shit out of you.'

One of the few high points of the tour came with the chance to record at Chess Studios, in Chicago. To Mick and Keith, this was sacred ground, and visiting it represented something of a pilgrimage. More unbelievable still was to find themselves surrounded by R&B greats like Chuck Berry, Willie Dixon, Buddy Guy and Muddy Waters, who shook their hands, offered advice and welcomed them into their extraordinary world. Spurred on by their most successful studio sessions to date, the band finished the tour well, with two sold-out shows at New York's Carnegie Hall.

The Stones made a triumphant return to Britain to discover that they had overcome the Beatles to be voted Best British Vocal Group in *Record Mirror's* annual popularity poll. Suddenly, they had made a leap in status from up-and-coming to full-blown pop stars. In July their new single, 'It's All Over Now' – a Bobby Womack song recorded at Chess – shot up the British charts to become their first Number One hit. On their next tour, beginning in July, audiences broke into a frenzy at almost every show, beginning with a 7000-strong capacity sell-out gig in Blackpool during which the audience caused £4000's worth of damage. Screaming girls were carried away in straitjackets from a gig in Belfast. Two policewomen fainted while attempting to control the crowds in Manchester. Fights broke out between bouncers and fans in Jersey. And so it went on.

By August, Stones Mania was reaching fever pitch. That month Marianne Faithfull, a virginal convent girl groomed for stardom by Andrew Loog Oldham, released her debut single. The song was 'As Tears Go By', a gentle ballad composed by Mick Jagger and Keith Richard, and it gave the songwriting partnership yet another Top Ten hit.

As the year progressed, the riots became predictable. The Stones could scarcely move on the streets without being mobbed. In the midst of all the madness, Charlie Watts married his girlfriend Shirley in October, two days before flying to Berlin to appear on a television show.

Before the end of that month, despite a schedule that had seen them almost constantly on tour since the beginning of the year, the Stones were back in America. This time, their British success followed them across the Atlantic. The road trip began with a first appearance on the prestigious *Ed Sullivan Show*, and during it the youthful audience went absolutely crazy. It was not a spectacle which Sullivan was keen to repeat. 'I promise you, they'll never be back on our show,' he said sternly. 'If things can't be handled, we will stop the whole business. We won't book any more rock'n'roll groups and we'll ban teenagers from the theatre if we have to . . .

LEFT: Marianne Faithfull was at Mick's side until the Sixties came crashing to an end.

It took me 17 years to build this show. I'm not going to have it destroyed in a matter of weeks.' Sullivan's nay-saying attitude had the effect of generating yet more publicity for the British boys.

The hysteria continued throughout the trip, reaching the height of notoriety when a misguided 17-year-old girl fell from a balcony at a gig in Cleveland. Meanwhile, back in Britain, the band's latest single, 'Little Red Rooster', had accrued advance sales of 300,000, ensuring that it would shoot straight to Number One in the week of its release. By the end of 1964, the Rolling Stones were well on their way to becoming the world's biggest rock'n'roll act.

GOOD TIMES

---

*'Future? Know something? I never even think
about it. Today's what counts. Ambitions?
Things are fine now. But I want to keep on
writing songs with Mick. It's a good
partnership, I think — we never seem
to be short of ideas.'*
KEITH IN 1966

FACING PAGE: *Mick and Keith's writing parnership showed
little promise until 1965.*

BY 1965 the Stones had achieved much of what they had set out to do. Along with the Beatles, they were the most celebrated party-guests on swinging London's fashion circuit. Despised by the Establishment for their music and looks, they were idolized and

---

'I don't think the Stones are more popular than Shakespeare, but he's been going longer.'
BRIAN

---

emulated by millions of British teenagers, while the youth of America was awaiting their return with bated breath. Mick Jagger was heard to predict that the band would probably last for another couple of years.

The Rolling Stones No. 2, recorded in London, Chicago and Hollywood, was released in January 1965, entering the charts – not surprisingly – at Number One. With the help of a choice selection of recent American R&B hits like the Solomon Burke classic 'Everybody Needs Somebody to Love' and the Gospel-tinged Irma Thomas track 'Time Is on

My Side', the Stones achieved their greatest ambition, seducing the British public with the animalistic beat of R&B.

Once again, the album's sleeve had only a posed portrait (by David Bailey) to indicate the identity of the artists. For the back, the mischievous Oldham had composed a nonsense biography written in the style of the fashionable bestseller *A Clockwork Orange* by Anthony Burgess: 'This is the Stones' new disc within,' he announced. 'Cast deep in your pockets for loot to buy this disc of groovies and fancy words. If you don't have the bread, see that blind man, knock him on the head, steal his wallet and lo and behold, you have the loot. If you put in the boot, good. Another one sold.'

These well-chosen words caused precisely the kind of public outcry that Oldham had intended. The matter was even raised in the House of Lords when a former Conservative minister took to the floor to claim that the record company should be prosecuted for 'a deliberate incitement to criminal action'. As the newspapers railed against the band's antisocial manifesto the records continued to sell, even after Decca had bowed under the pressure and withdrawn the offending sleeve.

RIGHT: *Like the Beatles before them, the Rolling Stones had become global stars.*

On January 21 the group arrived in Sydney for their first tour of Australasia, and were greeted by 3000 screaming fans. It seemed like nowhere on Earth was untouched by the band's wicked charm. By the time the Stones left, 30 days later, they had four records in the Australian Top Ten, including their throwaway cover version of the Drifters' 'Under the Boardwalk'.

But the year's most momentous event for them was the release of 'The Last Time', the first ever Rolling Stones single to feature a Jagger–Richard song on the A-side. At a time when everything seemed to be going their way, the public gave its seal of approval to the duo's songwriting talents by sending the single straight to the top of the British charts.

The band's dates for the rest of the year — and it was a heavy schedule — were selling out as fast as tickets could be printed. Two more weeks in Britain were followed by a tour of Europe and then, four days later, on April 22, they flew to Montreal for another North American trip. Despite the host's previous hostile remarks, the Stones made a triumphant return to the *Ed Sullivan Show*, where they performed 'The Last Time', currently at Number Eight in the

'America? Their way of thinking can be as antiquated as our standard of living.' KEITH

ABOVE: The men behind the scenes — Loog Oldham (left), Davis and Calder (right).

melody to tape. 'In the morning, I still thought it sounded pretty good,' he says. 'I played it to Mick and said 'The words that go with this are "I can't get no satisfaction". That was just a working title. It could just as well have been "Aunt Millie's caught her left tit in the mangle". I thought of it as just a little riff, an album-filler. I never thought it was anything like commercial enough to be a single.'

Returning to RCA Studios in Hollywood, everyone — except Keith, who had his doubts — agreed that '(I Can't Get No) Satisfaction' was the most exciting record that the Stones had ever made. Delivering an almost spoken pop vocal with deceptively sexual allure, Jagger's snarling voice was backed by Richard's unforgettable riff, played through a Gibson fuzz-box. While the tour continued, the single was rushed into American record stores, three months before its British release. Within two weeks it had jumped 60 places in the charts and by June 15 it had become the Rolling Stones' first *Billboard* Number One hit.

In order to capitalize on the band's success in America, London Records also released a compilation of old album tracks and studio out-takes called *December's Children (And Everybody's)*. Moreover, the

Billboard chart, and four other songs. However, while Sullivan's memory might have been selective, the American public was not so quick to forget. As the band travelled from town to town, the authorities prepared for the onslaught with sensational paranoia. Many hotels refused to give the group bed and board, while police officers patrolled everywhere in their hundreds, marshalling the crowds before, during and after each performance.

In a hotel in Clearwater, Florida, Keith Richard woke up in the middle of the night with a simple riff echoing in his head. Before he went back to sleep, he grabbed his guitar and committed the band's next album was released in America well before its British debut: *Out of Our Heads*, recorded entirely at the RCA Studios in Hollywood, exhibited some of their tightest studio work to date, although it was dismissed by some

---

'Suddenly it's all over. The curtains close quickly, shutting off the faces behind that ear-splitting roar. Back in the dressing-room, we swallow Cokes to get that sandpaper taste out of our throats. We start to unwind as we wait for the police to arrange our getaway.'
BRIAN

---

critics who had been hoping to hear disposable pop.

Back home, while the Stones were busy creating a legend in America, Oldham was still intent on turning himself into a one-man music industry. Unceremoniously ousting the band's long-serving agent Eric Easton, he went into partnership with hard-bitten American accountant Allen Klein. Klein's reputation in the music business was extraordinary – for example, his ability to dissect contracts and work financial miracles had earned Sam Cooke an unprecedented $1 million advance in 1964. Klein's list of American clients included Bobby Darin, Steve Lawrence and Bobby Vinton, but his British clients were the most successful: the Animals, Herman's Hermits, the Dave Clark Five, Donovan and others. The Stones, who had been tacitly dissatisfied with their contract for some time, were impressed by Klein's dynamic aura, despite his appearance. 'We all went down to the Hilton with Andrew to meet him,' remembers Keith. 'In walks this little fat American geezer, smoking a pipe, wearing the most *diabolical* clothes. But we liked him. He made us laugh. And at least he was under 50.'

While *Out of Our Heads* was Number One in America and 'Satisfaction' was topping the charts in Britain, Allen Klein was renegotiating the band's contract with Decca from the strongest possible bargaining position. He walked away from this meeting with $1.25 million advanced against royalties, and the promise of £3 million over the next five years.

ABOVE: The Stones toured constantly to maintain their place at the top.

Nevertheless, there was little time for the band to enjoy these riches. The touring continued: Scandinavia, West Germany and Austria, followed by another sold-out 22 dates around Britain, as wild as ever. At a show in Manchester on October 3, 1965 the police had to form a human barrier to protect the Stones from the surging throng; even so, Keith Richard was struck on the head by a projectile thrown from the crowd, and was out cold for five minutes.

As the British tour reached its conclusion, another Jagger–Richard composition was at the top of the *Billboard* chart: the upbeat and antagonistic rant, 'Get Off of My Cloud'. As the Stones set off yet again for America, the single was working its way to the top of the British charts, where it would remain for three weeks. In America Keith suffered once more when he accidentally touched a live microphone with his guitar and received an electric shock which put him out for seven minutes.

Later that evening, invited to a party in Los Angeles hosted by fashionable author Ken Kesey, Keith and Brian were offered their first taste of a volatile recreational drug so new that the authorities had not yet seen fit to prohibit it. The drug was called lysergic acid diethylamide – otherwise known as LSD or acid – an hallucinogenic drug which was destined to imprint itself on every aspect of popular culture for the next half-decade. Its effect was known as a 'trip', a period of blurred consciousness lasting as long as 24 hours, during which the user would be unable to distinguish objectively between fantasy and reality. At that time, cocaine – an addictive narcotic which was used legitimately as an anaesthetic but manufactured illegally as an 'upper', boosting one's energy and raising the heart-rate – was the recreational drug of the fashionable jet-set. The arrival of LSD, emanating from California, provoked a new wave of 'experimental' drug use by artists, musicians, writers and their followers. The Stones, no less than any other high-profile rock band, found their eyes being opened to the dawn of 'psychedelic' music-making.

The American tour ended in San Diego where, among the crowd of 14,000 fans, was German film star and fashion model Anita Pallenberg. She and Brian Jones had been romantically linked several times in the press after their first meeting at a gig in Munich. A former art student who had grown up in Rome, she was still only 23 years old but had lived in Germany, Britain and America and was fluent in four languages. To Pallenberg, Jones seemed funny, talented and unpredictable. To Jones, on the other hand, his latest girlfriend was the ultimate accessory to a successful lifestyle. He had the money, the fame and the trinkets – including a magnificent Rolls Royce Silver Cloud purchased from his friend George Harrison. All that had been missing from his life so far had been

a beautiful, high-class blonde on his arm. But in fact, although it lasted some while, their love was fated from the first, primarily because of Jones's own character deficiencies. Through a long line of failed relationships he had won women over with his soft-spoken charm, only to torment them – mentally and physically – and then cast them away with ruthless spite. A shallow, selfish man, he had cut

BELOW: 'Experimental' drug use ushered in a new era of music and fashion.

himself off from the mothers of his three children and indulged himself in the adoration of starstruck teenage fans.

As the Stones became ever more successful, Brian's selfishness was compounded by fits of depression and a

---

'Keith was my friend from way back, but he was also close to Brian, which was great for the band. However, there were terrible periods when everyone was against Brian, which was stupid, but then on the other hand Brian was a very difficult person to get on with and he didn't help.' MICK

---

steadily increasing dependency on drugs and alcohol. At home he slept through the day and never ventured out until after dark. In keeping with his rampant lifestyle, he was swallowing handfuls of amphetamines, washing them down with a daily couple of bottles of whisky. On tour he had been taken ill on a number of occasions as a result of drug-related

exhaustion, and for the same reason he had failed to appear at several studio sessions, including the recording of 'Satisfaction' in Hollywood.

His depression went hand-in-hand with paranoia. In the early days Jones had seen himself as the leader of the Rolling Stones. For a long time he had been paid more than the others and had even, when they were out on the road, arranged to stay in better hotels than the rest. However, as the Jagger–Richard songwriting partnership proved more and more fruitful, Brian's control over the band's affairs seemed to be slipping away. He began to feel that the other four were squeezing him out – and to an extent this was true. Trapped in a vicious circle, Jones was using drink and drugs to blot out his fear of rejection, but in so doing he was succeeding only in further alienating his friends.

Success for Jagger and Richard continued effortlessly. 'As Tears Go By' – the 1964 British hit which Jagger and Richard had written for Marianne Faithfull – was restyled as a Stones number, and at the start of 1966 it reached Number Six in the American charts. In February the band released '19th Nervous Breakdown', a fast and twisted blend of Country and

R&B; the song was a satirical poison arrow aimed at the facile neuroses of upper-class girls, featuring the self-righteous line 'It seems to me that you have seen too much in too few years'. Once again, the single reached the top of the charts on both sides of the Atlantic.

The next album, released in April 1966, was the most significant of their career. Dispensing with R&B cover versions, Jagger and Richard compiled 14 original songs to create *Aftermath*. (Originally the album was to have been titled *Can YOU Walk On The Water?*, but Decca – tired of the Stones' controversies – vetoed the idea.) Jagger at last gave vent in his lyrics to his personal emotions and prejudices, particularly in the opening track, the suburban nightmare 'Mother's Little Helper' (a vignette about a modern housewife whose comfortable life has sapped away her will to survive). 'Lady Jane' was a little harder to decipher (most likely it was a teasing schoolboy reference to *Lady Chatterley's Lover*), but 'Under My Thumb' was widely believed to be an unsubtle jibe at his crumbling relationship with Chrissie Shrimpton. Musically, the album broke new ground with 'Goin' Home', a Blues

jam which trampled on the conventions of pop music by rambling on for over 11 minutes.

Brian Jones was the star of this album – toying with unusual instruments, like the sitar, dulcimer (a stringed instrument that is a type of zither, given to him by an American folk singer) and marimbas – and thereby reminding the others of his surprising aptitude for musicianship. This experimental sound was a little before its time . . . and, sadly, time was running

ABOVE: The heart of the Stones is – and always has been – the Blues.

'*Brian was a dreamer.*' BILL

ABOVE: By 1966 the Stones had lost touch with their fans and their musical roots.

out for Brian Jones. His contribution to the music of the Stones was dissolving in direct ratio to his growing drug habit. His relationship with Pallenberg had lifted his spirits temporarily. Just having her around boosted his ego: he could flaunt her cosmopolitan beauty, intelligence and quick wit in the faces of his four friends. But in time his paranoia and violent temper eradicated any chance of maintaining that relationship. The next 12 months would be the beginning of the end of his life.

Aftermath topped the charts in Britain and America, although the band's most significant release of the year was 'Paint it Black', a dark, bass-heavy track featuring a sitar melody adroitly played by Brian Jones and a moody vocal from Jagger that ranged from ominous whisper to angry scream. A haunting gypsy curse (curiously and provocatively punctuated on the sleeve as 'Paint it, Black') reminiscent of 'The House of the Rising Sun' – which had been a hit for the Animals in 1964 – it was the group's first hit single to move radically away from their 'roots' in American R&B.

Individually, the band members sought stimulation from other sources. This was the time when the Flower Power movement was getting under way – an era of free love, spiritual reawakening and new concepts of popular music. Brian Jones was less and less entranced by the Stones, finding himself instead drawn to the mystic culture of Morocco, a country he visited with Anita Pallenberg to relax and study tribal instruments. Mick Jagger, although far more sensible and level-headed than Jones, was determined to live an overtly carefree lifestyle. His cosy relationship with Chrissie Shrimpton no longer fitted his jet-setting image and the couple split, with Jagger starting an ill-fated and public relationship with singer Marianne Faithfull, by this time already married and a mother. Meanwhile, Andrew Loog Oldham had become detached from the band, concentrating instead on his own Immediate Records empire, leaving business matters to Allen Klein and publicity to the Fleet Street PR veteran Les Perrin.

Despite all this, the band could not escape their commitments. After a brief summer break, they toured America and then Britain, playing to mobs of teenagers who drowned out the music with their screams and chants.

Early in 1967 the release of 'Let's Spend the Night Together' fanned the flames of notoriety once again, with its unforgivingly provocative refrain. The sexuality was too strong for the *Ed Sullivan Show*, whose producers insisted that Jagger replace the offending line with the words 'Let's spend some *time* together'.

The Stones finally overstepped the mark in Britain at the end of January when they appeared on the long-running television variety programme *Sunday Night at the London Palladium*. The finale of this show was the same every week:

'We shall never tour America again. It's very hard work and one bring-down after another . . . Every place you go there is a barrage of relentless criticism and after about the fourth week you just start lashing out.'
MICK IN 1967

---

the night's acts returned to the stage on a giant revolving platform, standing among large, cut-out letters that spelled the show's title, and waving to the viewing millions. In a moment of petulance, Mick Jagger refused — on behalf of the band — to 'take part in a circus' and, despite the blandishments of his agent and the television producers, he declined to be swayed. For once public sentiment was wholeheartedly against the band:

challenging authority was one thing, but insulting Britain's best-loved institutions (not only the top-rated television show but the Palladium itself) was just too much.

In February, the Stones' fifth album, *Between the Buttons*, entered the British charts, but its performance showed a distinct drop in sales and it peaked no higher than Number Three. Another Jagger–Richard collection, its contents varied from peculiarly British throwaway pop ditties like 'Complicated' and 'Cool, Calm & Collected' through the controversially drug-related 'Connection' to the distorted R&B thrill of 'Please Go Home'. It was something of a mixed bag, and the tunes were never to become live favourites; all but the embittered ballad 'Yesterday's Papers' were dropped from the band's repertoire for the forthcoming tour of Europe.

It was in 1967 that the Rolling Stones were forced in real life to face up to the British Establishment which they had been insouciantly baiting for so long. The previous year a journalist from a Sunday newspaper had encountered Brian Jones in the fashionable London nightclub Blases, in Kensington. During the conversation the imprudent Jones had confessed to regular experimentation with drugs. In February 1967 the story was reported in the *News of the World*. Due to ignorance, the writer unfortunately jumbled the facts, so that the article named the wayward Stone not as Jones but as Jagger. Jagger immediately reacted by appearing on television to refute the charges and threatening the newspaper with legal action. In turn, the *News of the World* retaliated by launching a quest to prove that Jagger was every bit the drug fiend they had suggested.

By coincidence or otherwise, just a week later the police were given an anonymous tip that Keith Richard's beautiful home – Redlands, in West Wittering, Sussex – was being used as a haven for the taking of illicit drugs. Swooping on the property in full force, the authorities discovered Mick Jagger, Keith Richard, Marianne Faithfull and friends relaxing around the television after a day in the country. In truth, everyone present had been tripping on acid throughout the afternoon, including Beatle George Harrison and his wife Patti, who had fortuitously left early and so avoided meeting the gatecrashers. However, although there was a large quantity of LSD on the premises, the police failed to discover it and found little to incriminate Keith Richard. After a search of the property they seized drug paraphernalia, some amphetamine tablets from Jagger's coat and some heroin belonging to a friend, London gallery-owner Robert Fraser, but no charges were immediately preferred. They then made their exit, leaving the company in a state of shock. 'Poor Mick,' Marianne Faithfull later recalled. 'He could hardly believe his bad luck. The first day he ever dares take an LSD trip, 18 policemen come pouring in through the door.'

Tensions within the band grew worse during the Rolling Stones' short break in March. With 'Ruby Tuesday' topping the American charts, Jagger, Robert Fraser and photographer Michael Cooper flew to Morocco, while Jones, Richard and Pallenberg followed on by road, driving across Europe in Richard's luxurious sky-blue Bentley Continental. During the road trip Jones was suddenly taken ill with a severe attack of asthma. In hospital, he was diagnosed as having acute pneumonia; at his insistence the other two carried on to Tangier without waiting for him.

During the course of that trip, Pallenberg and Richard began an affair. When Jones finally arrived at the Hotel Minzah, he was full of suspicion, and took out his frustration in private by beating Pallenberg into a stupor. When the beatings continued, Pallenberg went to Richard, sobbing that Jones was going to kill her and – while the offending Stone was busy in the town – the two lovers jumped into their car and headed north to Madrid, where they caught a plane to London.

BELOW: Anita Pallenberg drove a wedge between Keith and Brian.

'There was extra hassles between Brian and me because I took his old lady. You know, he enjoyed beating chicks up. Not a likeable guy. At the same time, he had a certain charm. And we all tried at certain times to get on with him, but then he'd shit on you. It sounds like I'm just putting him down, but I want to tell you the truth about this. You ask anyone else in the Stones and if they're honest they'll say the same thing.' KEITH

When he discovered that he had been abandoned without so much as a goodbye note, Brian Jones was crushed. Losing his girlfriend to Keith Richard seemed to confirm all of his paranoid suspicions that the rest of the band were conspiring to exile and humiliate him . . . but, of course, yet again the band's personal squabbles could not make their professional obligations disappear.

After Richard, Jagger and Robert Fraser had returned to Britain they were summonsed to appear in court on charges related to the Dangerous Drugs (Prevention of Misuse) Act (1964), but at the end of March the Stones were back on the road again for a three-week tour of Europe. Thanks to the publicity surrounding the drugs bust the band was hassled by Customs at every stop, so the trip was even more stressful than usual. In mid-April Jagger lost his temper with officials at Le Bourget Airport, and was silenced with a punch in the face.

After years of being regarded as the voice of a generation, Jagger finally began to speak his mind. He remained vague about party politics: the issue which most mattered to a Stone in 1967 was the freedom of the individual. Accordingly, he implied that his own persecution was a manifestation of a blanket oppression of the youth of the day. 'I see a great deal of danger in the air,' he announced soberly to the *Daily Mirror*. 'Teenagers are not screaming over pop music any more, they're screaming for much deeper reasons. We are only serving as a means of giving them an outlet.'

The idea that the Stones were 'serving' anyone but themselves was, of course, ridiculous. After spending so long wrapped in the pampered cocoon of stardom, Jagger had swallowed Andrew

Loog Oldham's absurd yet seductive PR. The LSE student who loved music for music's sake had disappeared, and what was left was a pop star putting words into the mouths of a nation of kids whom he no longer knew nor understood. 'Teenagers of the world are weary of being pushed around,' he opined. 'They want to be free and have the right of expression; of thinking and living aloud without any petty restrictions. This doesn't mean they want to become alcoholics or drug-takers or tread down their parents. This is a protest against the system. I see a lot of trouble coming in the dawn.'

Little did he know that, as a result of his rather naive prophetic opinions, Jagger would bring down the full weight of society on his own head. The Establishment wanted to quash the outright rebellion of Britain's youngsters and desperately needed to find a scapegoat. In May 1967 all eyes turned towards a group of decadent, outrageous pop stars with long hair and 'dangerous' ideas – namely the Rolling Stones.

COMING DOWN AGAIN

'When I'm 33, I'll quit. That's the time when a man has to do something else. I can't say what it'll definitely be . . . but it won't be in showbusiness. I couldn't bear to end up as an Elvis Presley and sing in Las Vegas with all those housewives and old ladies coming in with their handbags. It's really sick.' MICK

FACING PAGE: In 1967, the Stones discovered the downside to fame and power.

WHEN Mick Jagger, Keith Richard and their friend Robert Fraser stood in the dock before the magistrates in Chichester on May 10, 1967 they pleaded Not Guilty to their charges under the Dangerous Drugs (Prevention of Misuse) Act (1964). They were released on £250 bail, and told they were to be tried by jury the following month. That same afternoon, police raided a

'As far as I know, Brian Jones never wrote a single finished song in his life; he wrote bits and pieces but he never presented them to us. No doubt he spent hours, weeks, working on things, but his paranoia was so great he could never bring himself to present it to us.' KEITH

London flat belonging to Brian Jones and confiscated for chemical analysis 11 different items, including methedrine, hashish and cocaine. Jones spent the night in jail and the next morning was, as had been the others, released on bail of £250. From that point on, his contribution to

the Rolling Stones reduced drastically. Reluctantly, his oldest friends turned their backs on him.

'We'd spend an awful lot of time trying to get through to Brian, trying to help him,' Keith insists. 'But we'd have it flung back in our faces. We were working night after night. If someone isn't pulling their weight after a while it becomes incredibly difficult.'

With the threat of imprisonment hanging over their heads, the Rolling Stones made little headway in recording their next album. Jones had withdrawn into his own private, night-time world, experimenting with drugs alongside his close friend Jimi Hendrix, the brilliant guitarist and stage performer from Seattle who had become a huge success in Britain. In the studio — if Jones remembered to make an appearance at all — his flashes of brilliance were rare. Broken-hearted at the loss of Anita Pallenberg, he began a relationship with another blonde model, Suki Poitier, whom he secretly abused and roughed up as if she were a rag doll. His life was in a downward spiral.

Jagger and Richard were likewise short on inspiration. Jagger had a vision of producing a new album for the Flower

Power generation in the mould of the Beatles' *Sergeant Pepper's Lonely Hearts Club Band*, which had been released in June. The Beatles had, in one fell swoop, risen from the ranks of mere pop stars to become 'great artists', and Jagger aspired to repeat that achievement. Unfortunately, his determination to leap aboard the bandwagon would result in what was no more than a thin pastiche of the Lennon–McCartney genius – *Their Satanic Majesties Request*.

All of this seemed of strictly secondary importance as Jagger and Richard once again arrived in court, on June 27. Their barrister was Michael Havers QC, a future Attorney-General. His defence of Mick Jagger comprised a two-pronged attack. First he explained that Jagger had purchased amphetamine tablets in Italy in order to alleviate tiredness at work. On returning to Britain he had called his physician to ask about the medicine, and had been advised to carry on taking it. This, according to Havers, was tantamount to a prescription. Second, Havers pointed out that Jagger had bought the tablets in good faith in a country in which their sale was completely legal, and emphasized that any crime had been purely accidental.

However, the members of the jury were not convinced. After five minutes of discussion they returned with a verdict of Guilty. When the court adjourned later that afternoon, Mick Jagger and Robert Fraser (who had changed his plea to Guilty on the advice of his lawyer) were taken away in handcuffs to spend the night in jail, waiting to be sentenced. Keith Richard, who was still on bail, was

ABOVE: The Stones had dabbled with drugs long before it became fashionable.

free to go home and await his trial the next morning.

During the proceedings the press had a field day. The counsel for the prosecution, Malcolm Morris QC, attempted to prove that Keith Richard had knowingly allowed his premises to be used for the consumption of illegal narcotics. To do so, Morris painted a picture of events at Redlands that sounded less like an

---

'We are not old men. We're not worried about petty morals.' KEITH IN COURT, JUNE 1967

---

intimate party than a Roman orgy. Much was made of the fact that 'Miss X' – unnamed in order to protect her identity, although the whole world seemed to know that she was Mick Jagger's lover Marianne Faithfull – had been dressed in only a fur rug when the police had arrived at Redlands. This hint of sexuality was dwelt on at length during the trial and, in a process of Chinese Whispers, rumours swept the nation that the police had interrupted Mick and Marianne *in*

flagrante doing something quite unmentionable with a Mars Bar.

Jagger and Fraser spent another night in Lewes Prison as the joint trial went on. Havers put up a sterling argument against the charges, putting Keith Richard in the witness stand to explain that, as he was such a hard-working musician, it was impossible for him to account for the activities of all the people who surrounded him, even at a party in his own home. Havers also pointed out that the comments made at the expense of 'Miss X' were inadmissible since she had been accused of no crime and was unable to defend herself in court. Furthermore, Richard asserted that the entire event had been engineered by the *News of the World*, the muck-raking Sunday newspaper, in an attempt to smear Jagger's public image. However, despite Havers's efforts, the jury returned another Guilty verdict. To the horror of all concerned, Richard was sentenced to one year in prison, Fraser was given six months, and Jagger was sent down for three months.

That night, the weight of the Establishment dynamically and inexplicably swung back in favour of the Rolling Stones. There was little hope for Robert Fraser – a self-confessed, albeit penitent, heroin addict — but, while Jagger was locked in his cell in Brixton Prison and Richard was taken to Wormwood Scrubs, the nation cried out in support of the punished pop stars. The very next day, Havers won the release of the two Stones on bail of £7000 each, pending an appeal, while outside the offices of the *News of the World* protesters were chanting 'Free the Stones!'

The most momentous championing of the band members came from a very unlikely source. An editorial published in *The Times* on Saturday July 1, 1967, written by the editor William Rees-Mogg, was titled (quoting Alexander Pope) 'Who Breaks a Butterfly on a Wheel'. The article was a level-headed lambasting of a judicial system which — in fear of losing its reputation — had abused its powers in order to make an example of two very minor miscreants. This, pointed out the usually uncontroversial editor, was no way to win the trust and cooperation of the younger generation. 'It should be the particular quality of British justice', he concluded, 'to ensure that Mr Jagger is treated exactly the same as anyone else, no better and no worse. There must remain a suspicion in this case that Mr Jagger received a more

severe sentence than would have been thought proper for any purely anonymous young man.'

Rees-Mogg's 'suspicion' was quickly recognized as fact. At his appeal, Jagger's conviction was upheld, but his sentence was reduced to a conditional discharge. At the same time, the tissue-thin case against Keith Richard was overturned. During a television debate that same day, hosted by Rees-Mogg, Jagger faced the Establishment — in the form of a bishop, a Jesuit priest and a member of the House of Lords — and portrayed himself as a martyr to the cause of human rights. Without the effort of releasing a new record, he had managed to achieve the

ABOVE: By now, Mick was the unchallenged leader and spokesman for the band.

same elevated position occupied by the Beatles, albeit by a different route: he was a spokesman for a generation who had suffered for beliefs that defied the status quo. Echoing the sentiments of Keith Richard's defence in court, Jagger piously told the world: 'People should be punished for crimes, not for the *fears* of society, which may be groundless.'

The band's response to these events was the Beatle-inspired single 'We Love You', rumoured to feature backing vocals from Lennon and McCartney themselves. A dreary psychedelic chant, the song was

BELOW: Brian was capable of genius, but allowed it to slip away.

ostensibly aimed at the fans who had supported them throughout their ordeal, but secretly it was an acid-dazed jab aimed at the authorities who had pilloried them. A short film was made to accompany the record; it featured Jagger dressed as the persecuted Oscar Wilde, Faithfull as Lord Alfred Douglas and Richard as the Marquess of Queensberry. The film was scheduled to be shown on the popular music programme *Top of the Pops* but, on viewing it, the BBC declined to go ahead with the transmission.

Brian Jones was unable to shrug off his drug charges so flippantly. Slipping further into notoriety at his own court case on October 30, he was found guilty of possessing cannabis and allowing his flat to be used for the smoking of the drug. For this he was sentenced to nine months' imprisonment. The following day, he was released from the Wormwood Scrubs prison on bail of £750, pending an appeal in December. In stark contrast to the flood of supporting letters and media protests that had followed the Jagger–Richards trial, Brian Jones was convicted without controversy. There was only one public protest of note, during which eight people were arrested – among them was Chris Jagger,

Mick's younger brother. The four other Stones remained silent.

The album which resulted from that year's chaos and litigation was *Their Satanic Majesties Request*, the misguided attempt to exploit the success of the Beatles' *Sergeant Pepper*. Andrew Loog Oldham had by now relinquished the job of producer – a role he had never been qualified to fill in the first place – and the development of the album had been largely dictated by Mick Jagger's self-inflated ego. On the most ornate and expensive record sleeve ever produced, Jagger held court in a wizard's hat before a quartet of minstrels from a medieval fantasy. Like *Sergeant Pepper* this was a 'concept album', in which the tracks were segued together with sound effects and vignettes, culminating in a full track of rambling night-club ambience entitled 'On With the Show'. Although it had its high points (the sweet violins and cellos of 'She's a Rainbow' and the storming chorus of '2000 Light Years From Home', written by Jagger during his night in Brixton Prison) and some new ideas (like Bill Wyman's first credited Stones song, 'In Another Land'), the album was less original and arresting than even their

> *'I don't think that rock'n'roll songwriters should worry about art. I don't think it comes into it... As far as I'm concerned, Art is just short for Arthur.'* KEITH

early albums of R&B covers. Where the ragged vitality of 'Come On' had been a sincere interpretation of their passion for music, *Their Satanic Majesties Request* came across as the work of over-stressed pseudo-intellectuals who had mischievous ideas about champagne revolutions.

Brian Jones, struggling to regain his health, had submitted to hospitalization, and was making some progress. At his court appeal his physicians described him as 'a frightened young man' who possibly had suicidal tendencies. He was released on three years' probation with a £1000 fine. He then celebrated his freedom with an all-night bender of booze and pills, which resulted in him being rushed to London's St George's Hospital. With the authorities scrutinizing his every move, any hope of sobriety on his part was at best tenuous. Jones was suffering a

'Studios are like airports. They're all the same. It's always a shock to me when I walk out of a studio and suddenly realize I'm in Jamaica, Munich, Los Angeles.' KEITH

LEFT: Beggars' Banquet was Keith's favourite Stones album.

complete nervous breakdown – and yet, despite the fact that he was attempting to pick up the pieces, in May 1968 the police once again raided his apartment and charged him with possession of cannabis. Once more Jones was lucky: at his trial the following September he got off with a slap on the wrist. In the meantime, though, his paranoia had deepened to the extent that he spent sleepless nights telephoning friends in desperate need of human comfort.

In the studio, *Majesties* had proved that Mick Jagger could not cope as a record producer. In February 1968 it was announced that he no longer wanted to be 'on two sides of the control-room window', and that American record producer Jimmy Miller would begin working with the band at Olympic Studios. Immediately the tide turned, and the group's next album was destined to be one of their best – and, indeed, Keith Richard's all-time favourite. But it was also, tragically, the last Stones album to feature Brian Jones.

The first hint of the greatness of the upcoming album came with the track released in advance as a single: 'Jumpin' Jack Flash' was a high-powered riff first picked out on a piano by Bill Wyman.

The single put the Stones back at the top of the charts once again in both Britain and America.

The album's release was held up for a while due to a petty wrangle with Decca over the artwork for the cover — Jagger wanted a photo of a toilet wall covered with (fairly innocuous) graffiti, but Decca flatly refused, claiming the picture was offensive and tasteless. The final compromise was a plain white cover with the title written in an invitational script, a design not a million miles from that for the sleeve of the Beatles' *White Album*.

Beggars' Banquet opened with the Stones' most irresistible dance record, 'Sympathy for the Devil', a rock epic infused with a Latin American beat and based on themes from Mikhail Bulgakov's fantasy novel *The Master and Margarita*. The other high spot was 'Street Fighting Man', an R&B stomper inspired by talk of revolution — although Jagger's lyrics consummately failed to offer any answers to the questions they posed. Some of the album's best material harked back to the early days. 'Prodigal Son', a traditional Gospel Blues reworked by Jagger and Richard, was a moving precursor to the later classic 'You Can't Always Get What You Want', and there was a Gospel tinge

also to the closing Bob Dylan-inspired 'Salt of the Earth', in which Jagger's lyrics admitted that he had lost touch with his humble origins and the ordinary, working people, who 'looked so strange'.

The album was launched at a luncheon — arranged by publicist Les Perrin — attended by numerous celebrities who were served a huge feast of Elizabethan dishes such as boar's head. The afternoon culminated in a staged custard-pie fight, started by Mick Jagger; this made all of the newspapers, just as intended.

LEFT: Like Brian, Mick was capable of greatness.

After a year and a half off the road the Rolling Stones were now long overdue for another tour, but visa regulations regarding convicted criminals made working abroad a virtual impossibility for the rest of 1968. Instead, it was decided they should host a spectacular musical television show – with a stylized circus theme – to satisfy those fans who could not see them play live. John Lennon, Yoko Ono, Eric Clapton, Jethro Tull, the Who, Mitch Mitchell, Marianne Faithfull, Taj Mahal and model Donyale Luna joined the Stones for a marathon concert that was filmed before an invited audience. After the exhausting show was over Jagger decided that while he was happy with most of the film the performance of the Rolling Stones themselves had been drab and substandard. The possibility of refilming the band's climactic sequence was explored, but in the event broadcasting of the film was shelved indefinitely.

Brian Jones, meanwhile, had bought a beautiful house, Cotchford Farm, in the Sussex countryside. It had been the family home of A.A. Milne in the 1920s, during which period he had written the much-loved stories of Winnie the Pooh and Christopher Robin. Moving away from London distanced Jones from the spotlight and took him out from under the probing eyes of the police (indeed, the authorities immediately switched their attentions to Mick Jagger, who was once again convicted of drug possession). However, the rest of the band knew that Jones's criminal record would prevent him from ever again being granted an American work permit. Despite their sympathies, Jagger, Richard and Watts drove to Cotchford Farm in May 1969 to ask Jones to resign from the band. By all accounts this was a civilized meeting, during which Jones indicated an interest in forming a new band to follow his own personal musical direction. A press release echoed this same sentiment; in it he claimed that 'the only solution was to go our separate ways, but we shall still remain friends. I love these fellows.'

Jones must have felt terribly let down, but as far as his acquaintances could see he seemed to cope very well with the split. He continued to put on the airs of a rock superstar, holding parties and decorating his home with plush furnishings, but his dreams of regaining past glories were castles in the air.

On July 2, 1969 Jones hosted a spontaneous party which was attended by a number of fair-weather friends. Late that night, he drowned in his own swimming pool.

The events leading up to that tragedy are still shrouded in mystery. At the post mortem the coroner found that Jones had drowned while under the influence of drink and drugs, yet it was never explained why – with so many people around him – he was not rescued. Jones was known to be a strong swimmer, and the coroner found no evidence of an asthma attack – so why did he die? According to biographer Geoffrey Giuliano, the cause was far more sinister than a mere accident. A number of building contractors who had been hired to renovate the cottage had crashed the party, and one unnamed reveller now claims that two of the drunken men took a dislike to the ex-Stone and, for a few thoughtless moments, held him under the water until he was dead.

Jones was buried in his home town, Cheltenham, with his own understated epitaph: 'Please don't judge me too harshly.'

The reaction of the other band members was one of utter shock. 'I am just so unhappy,' remarked Jagger. 'I really lost

something. I hope he is finding peace.' Although it had been planned long before, the vast free concert in London's Hyde Park on July 5 before a crowd of 300,000 people had a special significance beyond the introduction of the band's little-known new guitarist, Mick Taylor (formerly of John Mayall's Bluesbreakers).

ABOVE: Brian's death was no great surprise – but how did he die?

Captured for posterity by Granada Television, the gig was performed on a stage decorated with a huge blow-up colour photograph of Jones. Jagger, dressed in flowing white, interrupted the show to read a passage from Shelley's *Adonais* in memory of his troubled friend. As more than 3000 white butterflies were released from the stage over the awe-stricken crowd, the Stones seemed to have reached the end of an era, not realizing that further tragedy was just around the corner.

In August the band had yet another Number One in Britain and America with the sexually aggressive 'Honky Tonk Women', and shortly afterward they were at last back on the road again. This should have been the tour that restored their reputation as the greatest rock band in the world, but the end result was yet another of rock history's black marks. On December 6, 1969 the group arrived in Altamont, California, to play a vast open-air gig — with an audience almost twice as big as the Hyde Park show's had been. Even before the Stones took to the stage there had been trouble. The 'security' team consisted of a branch of the San Francisco Hell's Angels, a tough,

LEFT: The Hyde Park Show became an inspiring memorial.

'One thing Altamont taught us was not to try and do anything like that again. In any case, rock sounds better in a room with 200 people. It really does.' KEITH

redneck biker gang who had nothing but contempt for the 500,000-strong crowd of hippies. Anyone attempting to climb onto the stage was beaten back into the crowd by Angels wielding pool cues. During the guest slot by Jefferson Airplane, fans were being carried into the site's small Red Cross tent faster than the medics could treat them.

When the Rolling Stones finally appeared, the crowd went wild and the Hell's Angels retaliated by turning even wilder. During Jagger's rendition of 'Sympathy for the Devil' a young black man, Meredith Hunter, was murdered – fatally stabbed in the back – and carried away. The Stones were aware that something had happened, although from up on the stage it was difficult to tell exactly what. The show continued uneasily. At one point Keith Richard almost came to blows with one of the Angels, but it was not until the following day that the Rolling Stones discovered that four people (including the murdered Meredith Hunter) had died that day, 700 had been treated for drug-related illness and a further 98 had been taken to hospital with abrasions and broken bones. The events were recorded in the 1970 movie *Gimme Shelter*.

It was the end of the Sixties, both literally and in spirit. Rock'n'roll would never be quite the same again.

LEFT: After Altamont, every Stones tour was immaculately planned, yet utterly over-the-top.

YESTERDAY'S PAPERS

'People always want to know about your sex life. Why? Because they've got nothing else to talk about. Because they've got empty heads. Because stupid heads print it in newspapers. People like gossiping.' MICK

THE LAST Rolling Stones album of the 1960s, *Let It Bleed*, was a creative high point for the band, featuring classics like 'Midnight Rambler', 'You Can't Always Get What You Want' and 'Gimme Shelter' that would still be in their set-list 25 years later. However, the long-lasting appeal of that record served to mark the beginning of a 20-year period during which highlights were very rare.

'I'm not amazed that the band is still going, just amazed that they get anything together. That's our claim to fame.' CHARLIE IN 1970

'We're not going to stay in the South of France for a whole year, we're going on the road. I couldn't live in France for a whole year.' MICK

In the summer of 1970, the band's seven-year contract with Decca Records came to an end. In order to 'honour' their contractual obligation the band provided the company with one final song for release. The title of that song was 'Cocksucker Blues' and – predictably – Decca refused to release it.

The early 1970s showed some flashes of brilliance from the Stones, but the band was being drawn apart by other influences: sex and drugs had priority over rock'n'roll, but the truly overriding interest was money. Civil litigation had become a part of all their lives, tying up their finances in endless courtroom battles. Their one-time booking agent Eric Easton sued Allen Klein and Andrew Loog Oldham for breach of contract, while Oldham and the Stones were simultaneously suing Klein for withholding royalties. After parting company with Decca and Klein, the Stones formed their own label, Rolling Stones Records, with an exclusive distribution deal through Atlantic. Then, in order to escape British taxes, all five members of the band decided to quit their homes in Britain and move to the South of France: they were rock'n'roll's first-ever tax exiles.

The band's new headquarters became Nellcôte, Keith Richard's Roman villa on a hill overlooking Villefranche-sur-Mer, halfway between Nice and Monte Carlo.

Jagger was taking little interest in music any more, instead forging for himself a career as a film star. He took a lead role alongside Anita Pallenberg, Michèle Breton and James Fox in Nicholas Roeg's controversial art-house movie *Performance* (1970), then starred in the disastrous Australian biopic *Ned Kelly* (also 1970). Meanwhile, his relationship with Marianne Faithfull had disintegrated. The young singer and actress whom Andrew Loog Oldham had promoted as a chaste beauty had grown sick, suicidal and ugly from her addiction to hard drugs. She and Jagger had been staying together more out of habit than anything else; when she finally decided to leave he went straight into the arms of the beautiful actress Marsha Hunt. A short while later he moved on again – leaving Hunt pregnant – to marry the Nicara-guan beauty Bianca Pérez Mora Macías, the daughter of an ambassador. On her wedding day Bianca Jagger was four months pregnant.

Jagger immediately began to live as a Paris socialite, following the same sort of

RIGHT: On the dance floor – Anita Pallenberg (Left) and Bianca Jagger (Right).

'*There's not going to be a wedding this week, next week or ever. Mick and I are very happy together. We don't need to get married. Why should we?*' BIANCA

'That was a load of shit. I only made it because I had nothing else to do.'
MICK ON *NED KELLY.*

'All that stuff you read in the papers about me and Bianca, it's like a page out of someone else's life. It has no relation to me at all. It's completely made up.' MICK

lifestyle he had so successfully cultivated in swinging Sixties London. The band seemed to be little more than a distraction from his party-going existence. Meanwhile, Keith Richard and Anita Pallenberg, who already had a son, Marlon, were struggling against a life-draining addiction to heroin; despite their efforts to kick the habit, they were constantly surrounded by music-business drug pushers and hangers-on who made the temptation almost impossible to resist. Pallenberg managed to kick the drug in a Swiss clinic long enough to give birth to a healthy daughter, Dandelion, but thereafter the dependency continued to eat away at her mind. Without a live-in nanny, the children often lacked even the most basic care as the two lovers wasted their days away, living to experience that blood-tingling rush. And, as the decade rolled on, the parents' relationship began to deteriorate.

They were not the only couple in trouble. The relationship between Bianca and Mick Jagger was doomed from the start because he was never prepared to put her before his career. Although he idolized his daughter Jade, his adoration of Bianca soon ebbed away. They began to lead separate lives, he travelling the world with his customary cool abandon while she wowed the fashion world with her daring clothes and Latin American beauty.

In 1972 the Stones' idyll in the French Riviera came to a sudden end. The police – who had been watching Nellcote for 13 months – finally swooped in December while the band was away from home in Jamaica, recording the new album, and court summonses were issued. As a result, Keith Richard was forced to pay a large fine but, despite damning evidence against the band's whole entourage, the others effectively escaped prosecution by leaving their homes behind and remaining in Jamaica.

Although Mick rallied round to support his wife when her family were among those stricken by a massive earthquake in Managua, their marriage was already a thing of the past. She resented the fact that her husband failed to provide a stable home for their daughter, always flitting from one country to the next to stay one step ahead of the tax laws. He, on the other hand, accused her of using his fame and status to make a name for herself as a model and film actress. Whenever the time came to make a choice – something Jagger always did his best to avoid – he would choose the band over the woman.

The heroin casualties in the Stones camp continued to build up, the next victims being guitarist Mick Taylor and his wife. After reluctantly following the band to France in 1971, Taylor had been a loyal, imaginative and stable force in the Stones' music, but he was in above his head. By 1974 it was clear that the only way Taylor could escape his growing drug habit was to get away from the Rolling Stones.

It took Keith Richard and Anita Pallenberg much longer to realize that a separation was the only answer. In 1973 they had once again been busted for possession, this time in London. Richard was discovered at home with not only cannabis and heroin but another of his favourite little toys, an illegal Smith & Wesson revolver and the ammunition to go with it. He escaped, yet again, with a fine.

'I never had a problem with drugs, only with cops.' KEITH

On March 26, 1976 Richard and Pallenberg had a third child, a boy they named Tara, in memory of their friend Tara Browne who had died tragically young. By a terrible irony, the baby was dead ten weeks later, from influenza. The couple were deeply shocked, and Pallenberg suffered a severe nervous breakdown. Later that year, while on tour in Britain, Richard crashed his car

'I got married for something to do. I thought it was a good idea. I've never been madly, deeply in love. I wouldn't know what it feels like. I'm not really an emotional person.'
MICK IN 1976

on the M1 motorway and, when a policeman arrived to help him, was arrested for possession of LSD and cocaine. Amazingly, when the case came to court in January 1977, he was released with just another fine – he even managed to prove himself sufficiently 'clean' to earn a further work permit for America.

However, when he was in Toronto the following month, the authorities raided his hotel room and he was found to be in possession of pure heroin worth £2500. Charged with the intention to traffic in illegal drugs, he faced a maximum penalty of life imprisonment. His trial date was set for October 1978, and in the interim he and Anita travelled to America to undergo neuro-electric acupuncture, a course of painful treatment designed to break their drug addiction once and for all. Yet again, Richard was lucky: his Canadian court case resulted in a probationary sentence – coupled with a promise to play a benefit concert for a local charity. However, he and Pallenberg finally realized that they could not survive if they remained together. Drugs had erected a barrier between them, and it was one they had maintained for ten years. Their best plan was to separate and hope that, one day, the barrier might fall.

LEFT: Despite a typically roller-coaster romance, Mick and Jerry Hall have been together for almost twenty years.

Meanwhile, the split between Mick and Bianca Jagger had become common knowledge. In the latter half of 1977, Mick was seen publicly with Jerry Hall, an awesomely tall 21-year-old Texan model who had been previously linked to Roxy Music's frontman, Bryan Ferry. Likewise, Bianca was walking out in the company of several famous men, including tennis star Björn Borg, actor Ryan O'Neal and Jack Ford, the son of the US President. She finally filed for divorce in 1978, claiming $12.5 million in settlement. Mick, never the most generous of ex-lovers, held up the legal proceedings for two years until Bianca finally accepted a mere $1 million.

All of which had very little to do with music.

Sticky Fingers, the first Rolling Stones album of the 1970s, was as provocative as ever; its sleeve, designed by Andy Warhol, featured a blue-jean-clad male crotch with an actual working zipper. The band's new logo was an equally lascivious statement of Warhol's commercial genius – a lolling red tongue protruding from between two thick, glossy, red lips. The model for the mouth was instantly recognizable.

The stand-out track, 'Brown Sugar', gave the world a chance to hear the wickedly sexual pillow talk that emanated from that moist-lipped mouth. Giving away just enough to titillate his audience, as always, Jagger crooned 'Brown Sugar, how come you taste so good?', and everyone seemed to know instinctively what he meant.

The extravagant back-to-the-roots follow-up, *Exile on Main Street*, came in May 1972, a double album for which Keith Richard was given much of the responsibility. Recorded in the basement of his Riviera home, it was made at a time when the guitarist was struggling every day with his addiction to heroin, yet he received very little help from Mick

ABOVE: Pop singer meets Pop artist; Mick with Andy Warhol in New York.

*'How come all the teenies ever wanna do is
tongue my diamond tooth?'* MICK

FACING PAGE: It wasn't until 1981 that the Stones got back on track.

Jagger, who was still casually enjoying his Parisian socialite existence. 'While I was a junkie,' Richard later boasted, 'I still learned to ski and I made *Exile on Main Street*.' The double album received mixed reviews on its release (despite reaching Number One in both British and American charts), but *Exile* has since been recognized as representing the Stones at something close to their finest. Opening with the carefree, sexually explicit stomp of 'Rocks Off', it includes only one British hit single ('Tumbling Dice'), yet all of the tracks seem to consolidate the sound of the Rolling Stones past and present – convincing white Gospel Soul ('Loving Cup', 'Let It Loose'), psychedelic rock ('Shine a Light') and Blues (the Stones' version of the traditional 'Stop Breaking Down'), plus a closing track that appears to bring all those influences together ('Soul Survivor').

In 1972, the Stones finally went back on the road once more. With a gigantic entourage and a huge stage set which they took with them wherever they went, they inadvertently set the standard for all superstar rock tours of the future. In fact, the expense of the tour was not an exhibition of extravagance, but rather an insurance policy against any recurrence of 1969's events in Altamont. Jagger in particular was secretly terrified that something could go wrong. As a result, the Stones travelled around North America in their own private Lockheed DC-7 jet (nicknamed *Lapping Tongue* after the Stones' logo on her side), followed, in articulated trucks below, by lights, scaffolding, sound equipment and road crew. Relations between Jagger and Richard were at this time strained. Richard's highs led him to increasing levels of puerile decadence – such as gleefully pushing a television set through a hotel window while being filmed by Robert Frank, who had been commissioned to make a documentary about the tour.

As their roving tax exile continued, the Stones recorded *Goats Head Soup* late in 1972, although the album was not released until eight months later. They had come to the Caribbean ostensibly to soak up the ambience of Jamaican music, but the resulting album instead reflected merely the individual band-members' stressful private lives – flashy, drab and directionless. Only Mick Taylor really shone, in tracks like 'Silver Train' – a solid, rootsy Blues in which his slide guitar virtuosity was reminiscent of Brian

Jones's in his heyday — and '100 Years Ago', in which his funky solo deftly transformed a heartless melody into something far more memorable. Controversy still prevailed — first there was the cover photo, by Mick's friend David Bailey, in which the singer's face was given a *de rigueur* look of androgyny, and second there was the song 'Star Star' (originally titled 'Star Fucker'), which used the slang word 'pussy' and caused flutters of anguish at Atlantic Records because of a line about 'giving head to Steve McQueen'. Sadly, the only track of lasting importance was 'Angie', a sad

BELOW: Bill has always insisted that he deserves more credit for the band's compositions.

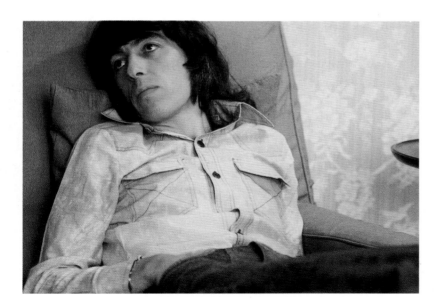

song of lost love and missed opportunities which was perhaps a reminiscence of Jagger's unhappy marriage and an expression of his rose-coloured memories of life with Marianne Faithfull. 'I felt close to this album and really put all I had into it,' claimed Jagger in reaction to critical disapprobation. 'But whatever you do it's always wrong. If you do it rocky, people say "Oh, it's just the same old rock-'n'roll" and if you do ballads, they say it's too pretty.'

In 1974, Bill Wyman became the band's first member to release a solo album: *Monkey Grip* was a flop, entering the British charts for only one week and peaking at Number 39. The band's own release that year, titled *It's Only Rock'n'Roll*, reached Number Two, but was commercially far from spectacular — despite the overblown album cover, which portrayed the Stones surrounded by elfin girls in a perverse parody of a *Broadway Melody* movie. Although the title track became a live favourite — it's a classic melody if you don't worry about the hackneyed sentiment — the album's only great track is its final one, 'Fingerprint File', a soulful epic in which Jagger adds a *noir*-ish vocal to Richard's seductively cinematic riff.

Mick Taylor departed that year, and the band used the studio sessions for their next album, *Black and Blue*, done in Munich and Rotterdam, to audition a number of possible replacements, including Wayne Perkins and Harvey Mandel (both of whom appeared on the finished record). However, when the Stones got word that Rod Stewart's band, the Faces, was about to split up, the job was offered to Faces lead guitarist Ronnie Wood. Woody, as he was affectionately known, had already contributed, in collaboration with Jagger, the original riff to 'It's Only Rock'n'Roll'. He was perhaps technically not the best guitarist around, but he had a feel for the music and an idiosyncratic style reminiscent of Keith Richard's. On the band's 1975 tour, Woody fitted in perfectly — as he has done ever since. It was a baptism of fire for the guitarist, who had to learn a 34-song set-list in three weeks before setting off in June on a 58-night tour of North America. But, looking at the two guitarists on stage today, it is hard to remember a time when Keith Richard's sparring partner was anyone else.

The first Rolling Stones album to feature Ronnie Wood was, though, yet another low point. As with the previous

effort, production on *Black and Blue* was credited to The Glimmer Twins (Jagger and Richard). The overall feel was glossy and clean, whereas once the Stones had been rough and dirty. The album was a misguided commercial reaction to the Soul-influenced disco pop of the day — giving the public what the Stones thought they wanted. It certainly succeeded financially, reaching Number Two in the British charts, but musically its high spot — the single 'Hot Stuff' — was merely a bland reworking of a very tired, raunchy rhythm.

The Stones seemed to be running out of steam.

ABOVE: Ron Wood (Right) with Rod Stewart in the Faces.

CONTINENTAL DRIFT

---

*'I'm not a kid anymore, and I've thought
to myself, 'How long can I keep doing this?'
But within the narrow confines of rock'n'roll,
it's for me to find out how to use my
experience and produce something that
hopefully is still worth listening to. Like I
said, somebody has got to find out how far
you can take this thing, and I guess it might
just as well be me!'*
KEITH

FACING PAGE: *No one, even the Stones themselves, knew that
the band's career would be so long.*

IN 1977 EMI picked up the rights to manufacture and distribute the 'independent' Rolling Stones Records label for the next six years. The first release under the new regime was *Love You Live*, a double album culled from the 1976 tour – an absurdly theatrical show which featured a giant inflatable phallus in the middle of the stage. Once again this was an album that failed to thrill.

The next album proper did not materialize until 1978, coinciding with the band's ninth American tour. *Some Girls* featured the American Number One (and British Number Three) hit 'Miss You', another track with a disco beat which defied the New Wave explosion and confounded the Punk upstarts, who were preaching doom for rock'n'roll's dinosaurs. Indeed, one of the album's other tracks, 'When the Whip Comes Down', seemingly an allusion to bondage chic, demonstrated the ever-adaptable Jagger picking up a guitar as if to illustrate the Punk Rock creed that you didn't have to be able to actually *play* in order to get up and make some noise. The album was best when it stayed on well-trodden territory. The title track stirred up the usual controversy with a supposedly ironic bit of sex talk ('Black girls just

want to get fucked all night'); 'Beast of Burden' was a conventional but pleasing Stones ballad; and 'Respectable' (which peaked at Number 23 in the British charts) was a peppy R&B track featuring a trademark Chuck Berry riff from Keith Richards (who had lately restored the 's' to his name). Conversely, the Country & Western 'Far Away Eyes' was so over the top it sounded like a novelty song.

ABOVE: Sometimes you don't know whether to laugh or cry.

The album was, nevertheless, an improvement over recent efforts, and it now seems all the more impressive given the band's next release, *Emotional Rescue*, in 1980. If little green men had landed on Earth wondering what our world's best-selling record was like they would have given us little credit for taste. Although *Emotional Rescue* made the customary run to the top of the British and American charts, it was a dud. The title track was no more than Stones-by-numbers, and the single drawn from the album, 'She's So Cold', was a dreary, repetitive drone. Only 'Down in the Hole', a simple, harmonica-infused Blues, could be counted a highlight.

Considering the group's personal lives, it was no surprise that the album was such a mess. Richards had finally split from Anita Pallenberg (following an incident in which a young man had committed suicide in her New York State apartment), Wyman had split from his second wife, Astrid (his first wife, Diane, had left him long ago, well aware of what went on backstage each time the Stones went on tour), Wood had already notched up his first arrest for possession (making him a Stone in word and deed), while Jagger was besotted with Jerry Hall, who would in due course bear him three children.

But 'Start Me Up', in 1981, was evidence of a band at last back on course. This was another in their unforgettable history of voyeuristic paeans to female beauty; it featured a chunky Richards guitar part and a pounding on-beat rhythm from Charlie Watts. The succeeding album, *Tattoo You*, was yet another mixed bag, but the single was enough to convince the public that the Stones were worth a further try.

The band hit the road one more time, beginning with a 'secret gig' before 350 people in Massachusetts before opening at Philadelphia's JFK Stadium in front of a sell-out crowd of 90,000. The group proved once and for all that, rather than being rock dinosaurs, they still enjoyed a popularity that would never die. Playing 50 North American cities in a mere three months, they performed for capacity crowd after capacity crowd. Five concerts in New York and New Jersey sold out within a matter of hours, to the chagrin of most of the four million fans who applied for tickets by post. Grossing $50 million, this was the most successful tour so far in rock-music history – but the Stones were only just getting started.

In 1982 they played 14 countries in Europe, ending up at Roundhay Park, Leeds, in July.

The money kept on rolling in during 1983, when the Stones signed yet another record-breaking contract, licensing their next four albums to CBS for a cool $25 million advance against royalties. Their CBS debut was *Undercover*, the first album by a renewed band – one that had transformed rock music into a gigantic, stadium-crumbling sonic boom, as indicated by the healthy sales of the recent live album *Still Life*. Featuring

---

'I think that rock'n'roll songs are pretty ephemeral . . . when I've done one I want to write another one.' MICK

---

the hard-funk title track 'Undercover of the Night', the album provoked the now expected controversy, the single's video promo climaxing in Jagger's being shot in the head by a Central American death squad.

A strong seller, *Undercover* gave the Stones pause for thought. For years they had collectively assumed that their careers would, in due course and perhaps in the not too distant future, come to a natural end. Although Jagger and Richards had never seriously planned for the future, they were both surprised to discover that, with their 40th birthdays drawing near, their band, the Rolling Stones, was more popular (and lucrative) than ever.

So, during the rest of the 1980s, the Stones went through a strange transition, learning to deal with their renewed and ever-growing popularity and at the same time searching for direction. Wyman was continuing to record his own material – always complaining that Jagger and Richards had denied him the writing royalties he deserved from the Stones catalogue. By 1985 he had released three albums and organized the *Willie & The Poor Boys* project (with friends Jimmy Page, Chris Rea, Ringo Starr and Charlie Watts) to raise money for ARMS (Action for Research into Multiple Sclerosis). Keith Richards had tried his luck on his own, touring with a band called the New Barbarians (also featuring Ronnie Wood) back in 1979, but was now occupied with his young wife Patti and their baby girl Theodora. Charlie Watts had assembled a 33-piece big band to dedicate himself to his great love of jazz and Blues. Finally came the turn of Mick Jagger, who in 1985 released his debut solo album, *She's the Boss*, to a lukewarm critical response.

The band's mid-life crisis came to a head with the shocking news, in December 1985, that their old friend Ian Stewart had died suddenly of a heart attack, aged 47. Although Stew had been dropped from the official line-up as far back as 1963, he had remained with them ever since as their faithful road manager and pianist. A friendly, reliable and trustworthy companion, his place could never be filled; nonetheless — or perhaps for this reason — when the band got together for a special, invitation-only concert in London to pay tribute to him they were filled with vitality. According to witnesses, the show at the 100 Club in February 1986 was the Stones' most dynamic performance in 20 years.

A month later their new single, a cover of the Sixties hit 'Harlem Shuffle' drawn from the album *Dirty Work*, was climbing the charts to reach the Top Ten in both Britain and America. Unfortunately, while Keith Richards was hungry to return to the road, Mick Jagger had other plans. He staunchly refused to support the album with a tour, preferring to concentrate on his solo career. Richards was furious that anyone should jeopardize the band's success, and the feud that developed between the two froze the band's efforts for nearly three years.

LEFT: Charlie is happiest when playing jazz.

Meanwhile Bill Wyman — traditionally one of the 'quiet' Stones — for the first time hit the headlines, and hit them with a vengeance. The *News of the World* broke the exclusive story that a 16-year-old called Mandy Smith had been living with the ageing bassist in his London flat for almost three years. The couple would be gossip-column fodder for years to come.

'The only things Mick and I disagree about is the band, the music and what we do.' KEITH

'Maybe Bill's happy running his restaurants and marrying people he never sees again. I don't know.' KEITH

Jagger's second solo album surfaced in 1987. *Primitive Cool* was not a big success, peaking at Number 26 in the British charts and failing to reach the Top Forty in America. A planned solo tour had to be postponed when guitarist Jeff Beck walked out on him, claiming to have been 'insulted' by the fee Jagger was offering. Furthermore, Jagger's song 'Shoot Off Your Mouth' was an undisguised attack on his long-time partner Richards . . . who soon retaliated with 'You Don't Move Me' on his debut solo album *Talk is Cheap*, which Richards promoted on a 15-date American tour.

The vendetta between Jagger and Richards was quickly terminated when concert promoter Michael Cohl, of the Canadian-based Concert Promotions International, offered the Stones the biggest deal in rock-music history. For a stunning $70 million the Rolling Stones would return to the road to play 50 concerts. Before this ground-breaking trip began, Jagger and Richards arranged to spend two weeks in Barbados in the hope of coming up with some new material. 'I told my wife I'd be back in either two weeks or 24 hours,' Richards later said, 'because I'd know in 24 hours if this thing was going to work or if

LEFT: Bill and Mandy were married in secret, but threw a big party in London three days later. Spike Milligan presented Bill with a walking-frame as a wedding gift.

we were just going to start cattin' and doggin'.' In fact, the result of the meeting surprised them both. The two Stones composed more than 40 songs, which they whittled down to 15 of the best for their new album. 'The songs just tumbled out,' reported Keith happily. 'First we screamed and yelled at each other. We needed to clear the air. Then we sat down with our guitars and something entirely different took over. You can't define it; it's something that always happens . . .'

Steel Wheels was the album no one had thought the band could ever make again. The Rolling Stones could not have recaptured the early days, but after many years of stumbling through the music-business mire they had remembered why they'd started the band in the first place. The album opened with four of the best tracks they had recorded in years: 'Sad Sad Sad' was a stomping, brass-heavy stadium anthem; 'Mixed Emotions' was the song that brought Mick and Keith back together again; 'Terrifying' was a high-octane funk jam with a brilliant, moody vocal; and 'Hold Onto Your Hat' sounded energetic and vivacious enough to have come from a band half their age. 'Rock and a Hard Place' became, for

obvious reasons, a single, although its melody was rather bland and contrived, but the lovely 'Almost Hear You Sigh' (originally destined for Richards's solo album *Talk is Cheap*) was the most memorable ballad to come from the Jagger–Richards collaboration since 1973's 'Angie'. Perhaps the most exciting piece,

---

'Even if we both said "I never want to see you again", we'd still have to deal with each other for the rest of our lives. There are too many businesses that demand our attention, too many people that depend on the salaries we pay them. It's like a marriage with no divorce.' KEITH

---

and for the band the most liberating, was 'Continental Drift'. In order to produce the lengthy instrumental section, destined to open proceedings on their forthcoming tour, they visited Tangier to record the strange and hypnotic sounds of the Master Musicians of Jajouka, a traditional troupe 'discovered' by Brian Jones more

'We're not an old married couple who can't live together and can't live apart; we're two men who've been friends for 30 years. Occasionally you want to strangle even the closest of friends.' MICK IN 1989

than 20 years earlier. Jones had always harboured an ambition to take the music of this troupe to the rest of the world — indeed, he had been visiting the Master Musicians on the very day that Keith Richard had run away with Pallenberg, leaving him in Morocco alone.

The 1989 tour was, once again, the most successful of all time to that date. Three hundred thousand tickets (priced $28.50 each) for the four bookings at New York's Shea Stadium sold out in a few hours. The stage was the band's most extravagant ever — almost 91m (300ft) in length, with bright orange cat-walks, 15m (50ft) inflatable dolls and incredible pyrotechnic effects. After witnessing two-and-a-half hours of greatest hits combined with moments from their best album in years, everyone was in

agreement: the Rolling Stones really did know how to put on a show.

After playing 61 gigs in 31 cities before a total of 3.2 million fans, the Stones had already raked in over $100 million; but, not content with breaking every record in the book, they carried on. Fourteen sold-out nights at the Korakuen Dome in Tokyo, Japan (another $30 million in revenue) were only the precursor to the Urban Jungle Tour of Europe in 1990, when the band played 45 nights between May and August.

Ending their relationship with CBS with the now obligatory concert album, *Flashpoint*, the Stones were once again

Below: The Jagger/ Wood/Richards partnership is now the Stones' core.

free to sell themselves on the open market. As luck would have it, Virgin Records boss Richard Branson was planning to sell his record business but felt that he needed a *really* big-name act on his roster if he were to attract the attention of buyers. This in mind, he was prepared to pay through the nose to get the Rolling Stones. In a deal worth $45 million for just three albums, the Stones signed to Virgin in November 1991.

In private, the lives of the Stones were as eventful as ever. Bill Wyman's debacle with Mandy Smith hit boiling point when he married her, she aged 19 and he aged 52, in 1989. The press were happy to say 'I told you so' in November 1990 when it was announced that the couple had already separated; it had been a marriage impossible to maintain under so much public scrutiny. In April 1993, once out of the spotlight again, Wyman married his fourth wife, the American fashion designer Suzanne Accosta. While working on his new solo album *Stuff* he announced, not for the first time, that he had left the Rolling Stones. The difference was that this time it was true.

Mick Jagger, meanwhile, became a grandfather, finally married his long-time lover Jerry Hall, had a leading support

'*We'll miss Bill, but I don't think it will faze us that much. We'll get someone good, a good dancer.*' MICK

'*You can't keep it up with sixteen-year-old girls forever. They're very demanding.*' MICK

'Charlie Watts is my absolute favourite. He has all of the qualities that I like in people. Great sense of humour, a lovely streak of eccentricity, a real talent, very modest. The only thing about Charlie that's always been true is he's always hated being a pop star.'

KEITH

been followed up most recently by *Warm and Tender* (1995).

After a lengthy hiatus – and for the first time without Bill Wyman – the Stones congregated at Woody's 17th-century farmhouse in Ireland's County Kildare to begin rehearsals for a new album. Moving on to U2's Windmill Lane Studios in Dublin in October, they recorded *Voodoo Lounge* with legendary producer Don Was and guest bassist Darryl Jones. At the time, hard-rocking

role in the mainstream science-fiction film *Freejack* (1992), and completed a third solo record, *Wandering Spirit* (1993). Keith Richards also continued to work as a solo artist, releasing his second album, *Main Offender*, in 1992, touring with his band the X-Pensive Winos and bringing up his latest offspring, a daughter named Alexandra.

Both Ronnie Wood and Charlie Watts settled down in Britain with their wives, enjoying their comfort and indulging their hobbies as artists. Watts also continued to work on his jazz projects; his heartfelt *Tribute to Charlie Parker* (1992), released under the name of the Charlie Watts Quintet, was a success, and has

'I never wanted to do a solo record until I started doing it.' KEITH

guitar bands like Nirvana and Pearl Jam were restoring the credibility of old-timers like Neil Young and Iggy Pop, and so the moment was perfect for the Stones to make another big comeback. Don Was encouraged the band to play live in the studio, working as a unit to recapture the feeling of vitality that had been so obvious on their last world tour. The spectacular result won two Grammy Awards and was even better than *Steel*

ABOVE: The dynamic
Voodoo Lounge *stage.*

LEFT: *Jagger is as taut,*
energetic and virile now
as he was 15 years ago.

Wheels. The title and the obligatory 'Parental Guidance' sticker on the front cover were sure signs that the Stones had not gone soft in old age. 'You Got Me Rocking' had all the thrill of their Sixties heyday; 'The Worst' had a superb rhythmic groove, overlaid by Ronnie Wood's seductive pedal steel guitar and Richards's growling vocal; 'New Faces', a medieval-style ballad using harpsichord and recorder, harked back, without seeming too saccharine, to the Stones' one-time Flower Power influences, as did the romantic 'Out of Tears'; conversely, 'I Go Wild' was a punchy rant and 'Suck on the Jugular' was a hard-rocking funk jam. All 15 tracks glowed with success, from Woody's and Richards's distinctive Country guitar duets to Jagger's lyrical epics.

The ensuing world tour began on August 1, 1994 at the RFK Stadium in Washington DC. This was the band's biggest show to date, and featured a stage set that weighed 300 tons and was crowned with a vast snake which opened the concert by spitting out a tongue of flame 9m (30ft) long. The North American tour continued until December 18, Keith's birthday, and proved to be the biggest-grossing tour in history ($140 million), surpassing Pink Floyd's comeback and even the Stones' own *Steel Wheels* tour. Even after it was over, though, the work continued, with a 1995 European tour as the worldwide sales of *Voodoo Lounge* topped eight million. By the end of this marathon the group had

---

'We're no nightclub act. It's not the same every night. People say that a lot . . . People say [the Stones are] a self-parody of what they were ten years ago. I doubt whether they actually saw us ten years ago.' MICK

---

earned an estimated $400 million. No one could argue that the Rolling Stones had not restored their status as the greatest rock'n'roll band of all time.

The future for the Rolling Stones has seldom looked better. In 1995 fans were teased with the single 'Like a Rolling Stone', a version of the Bob Dylan song, issued to complement the live concert

album *Stripped*. Despite the lack of a new studio album, there has been a wide range of different band-related products. Thanks mainly to Mick Jagger's fascination with technology, the Stones have remained at the cutting edge of the 1990s. *The Stones at the Max*, a film documentary drawing on the *Steel Wheels* tour made in 1990, used a unique new film process to create an image which could be viewed only on a screen 30m (100ft) wide. Although the film could be viewed only in specially adapted theatres, it was an unforgettable spectacle, and a sign that the Stones were always going to be the first to try new forms of expression.

In 1994 that concept held good when they became the first major group to transmit a live concert over the Internet, a computer network which links together viewers throughout the world. Similarly, computers have played a big part in their recent output. The eerie concept of *Voodoo Lounge* was exploited in an interactive CD-ROM whereby fans could navigate their way around a spooky mansion in Louisiana, 'meeting' the band, watching their videos, and solving taxing puzzles to find out more about the band's world. Simultaneously, the Stones launched, once again via the Internet, *Stones World*, a computerized encyclopedia of the band's past, present and future that can be freely accessed. With a computer modem hook-up to *Stones World* the fans can discover fine artwork, a discography, interviews, a complete day-by-day history and video clips which have been superbly collected and designed (net surfers can find the site at http://www.stonesworld.com). Even *Stripped* has an element of computerized interactivity: although it looks like an ordinary CD, you can slip it into your PC or Mac to view video clips, lyrics to all of the songs, candid photos of the band and much more.

The Rolling Stones have grown from a ragged band of Blues fans into a huge, corporate rock empire. Despite the distractions of groupies, deaths, drugs, alcohol and misguided musical tangents, they have remained the greatest rock band in the world simply because, when they get up on stage, all the scandals fall away. What makes them so great, what keeps us coming back to see them every time, is their magnetic presence. The long-faced, sensible drummer punching out an irresistibly danceable rhythm; the thin, laconic guitarists, shooting sidelong glances across the giant stage while sporting cigarettes never far from the necks of their guitars; and the pouting, strutting frontman who can get away with anything. These are the diverse personalities who have captured hearts, minds and headlines for more than three decades.

They are not dinosaurs: they are entertainers who are as shocking and explosive as ever. How much longer they can keep going depends not on nostalgia but on novelty, and the Stones have never failed to come up with a new twist to their glorious brand of 'roots' rock'n'roll.

BELOW: The Stones being inducted to the Rock'n'Roll Hall of Fame (with Mick Taylor, left, replacing Bill Wyman for the honours).

DISCOGRAPHY

The Rolling Stones *(1964)* **The Rolling Stones No. 2** *(1965)*
Out of Our Heads *(1965)* **Aftermath** *(1966),*
Got Live If You Want It *(1966)* **Between the Buttons** *(1967)*
Their Satanic Majesties Request *(1967)* **Beggars' Banquet** *(1968)*
Let it Bleed *(1969)* **Get Yer Ya-Yas Out!** *(1970)* **Sticky Fingers** *(1971)*
Exile on Main Street *(1972)* **Goats Head Soup** *(1973)*
It's Only Rock 'n' Roll *(1974)* **Black and Blue** *(1976)* **Love You Live** *(1977)*
Some Girls *(1978)* **Emotional Rescue** *(1980)* **Tattoo You** *(1981)*
Still Life: American Concert 1981 *(1982)* **Undercover** *(1983)*
Dirty Work *(1986)* **Steel Wheels** *(1989)* **Flashpoint** *(1991)*
Voodoo Lounge *(1994)* **Stripped** *(1995)*

Recommended CD Compilations: Jump Back: The Best of '71–'93 *(1993)*
The London Years (three CD box set) *(1989)*